CONTENTS

WEIRD AND WONDERFUL
INVENTIONS

What's the difference between a great invention and a ridiculous idea? It's difficult to say. In 1876 people laughed at Alexander Graham Bell's new telephone. In the early 1900s people snickered at those strange "horseless carriages" that slowly sputtered down the road. And in the 1940s many people thought that TVs were a passing fad. But cars, telephones and TVs have all been incredibly successful inventions.

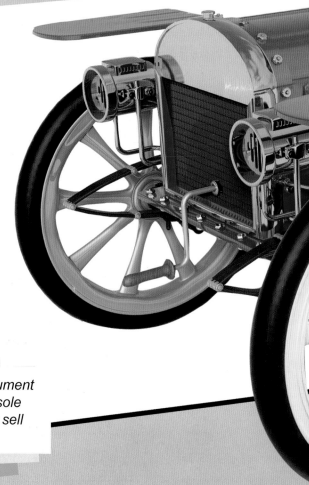

However, the chances of an invention succeeding aren't very good. Inventors have worked on many wacky ideas throughout history. Each year governments give hundreds of thousands of **patents** to inventors. But 99 per cent of inventors' ideas never actually make a profit.

patent *legal document giving someone sole rights to make or sell a product*

EARLY CAR, OR "HORSELESS CARRIAGE," FROM 1910

The great scientist and mathematician Albert Einstein once said, "If at first an idea is not absurd, then there is no hope for it." Read on to see how some people have taken Einstein's words to heart in the strangest ways.

CHAPTER 1

WEARABLE WACKINESS

Why learn how to tie a tie when you can wear one that zips up instead? How would you feel about wearing a T-shirt that also functions as a guitar? You never know what kind of wacky wearable invention will be the next big thing.

SMITTENS

One chilly day inventor Wendy Feller was going for a stroll with her husband. They tried to hold hands, but their bulky mittens ruined the romantic mood. That's when Wendy had the idea for Smittens. The **slogan** for these mittens for two says it all, "Hold hands. Stay warm. Love." Now couples can stay inseparable, even in the coldest temperatures.

slogan short catchy phrase used to advertise something or to sum up an idea

SOUND PERFUME GLASSES

Researchers in Japan have set out to give your social life a lift by developing special glasses. Sound Perfume glasses give off special scents and sounds when you meet new people. The glasses are also supposed to help you remember people's names. However, to work correctly, other people need to wear the glasses too.

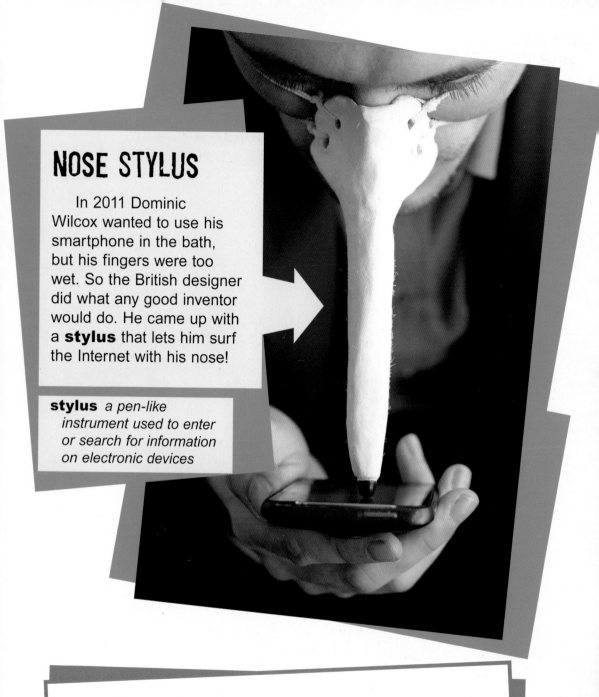

NOSE STYLUS

In 2011 Dominic Wilcox wanted to use his smartphone in the bath, but his fingers were too wet. So the British designer did what any good inventor would do. He came up with a **stylus** that lets him surf the Internet with his nose!

stylus *a pen-like instrument used to enter or search for information on electronic devices*

THE ZIPTIE

This "revolutionary" tie zips up just like a jacket. Other ties also use zips but hide them behind the tie's knot. However, the ZipTie turns the zip itself into a fashion statement!

TEMPORARY LIP TATTOOS

Do you fancy leopard-print lips? Temporary lip tattoos come in a variety of patterns. Choose from rainbows, polka dots, flags and more! These funky temporary lip tattoos work like stickers. They go on with water and can be removed with baby oil.

GAZE-ACTIVATED DRESSES

Designer Ying Gao's hi-tech dresses demand to be looked at – literally. Eye-tracking technology inside the fabric sets off tiny motors that make the dresses wave and wiggle when people look at them. The more people stare at the dress, the more it squirms.

WOODEN SWIMMING COSTUMES

Roll out the barrels! In 1929 some people actually wore swimming costumes made out of wood. They were supposed to help people float in the water – if they could put up with the splinters!

SNOWSTORM FACE PROTECTORS

In the 1930s people braved blizzards with heavy coats and thick wool scarves. But the scarves could be very itchy. In 1939 someone tried to solve this problem with plastic snowstorm face protectors. People could watch as snowflakes slid off the see-through cone. They worked well at first, until your breath misted it up – or you ran out of oxygen!

amplifier piece of equipment that changes sound or makes it louder

ELECTRONIC GUITAR T-SHIRT

The guitar graphic on this T-shirt is actually playable! Buttons along the neck play major chords. To "strum" the guitar, just rub a coin across the bottom of the guitar image. This amazing invention even comes with a mini **amplifier** so that everyone can hear you playing your t-shirt.

EYE SCREENS

Imagine what it would be like to read words from your eyeballs! A Belgian researcher is attempting to develop "smart" contact lenses that include built-in screens. These special lenses could be used as sunglasses, to read private messages, or even to change your eye colour.

10

AMAZINGLY REALISTIC FACE MASKS

Next Halloween spook your friends by going – as yourself! For roughly £2,500 a Japanese company will make a mask of your face that's incredibly life-like. It even simulates the blood vessels inside your eyes. The mask combines photos of you from every angle, and then stretches the image over a 3-D mould of your face.

ELECTRIC FACIAL MASK

"Rejuvenique" was a real hit in the late 1990s. Makers of the battery-powered mask claimed that people could have more youthful looking skin. Tiny electrical shocks were supposed to tone facial muscles under the skin. But the truly shocking part was how creepy the mask looked!

CHAPTER 2
HI-TECH HEAD-SCRATCHERS

Successful inventions usually solve a problem or meet a need. But some inventions do strange things, such as putting designs on toast or letting dogs send text messages. Some inventions prove that just because people can do something, it doesn't always mean that they should.

DIGITAL TATTOOS

People can now have tattoos that change with the wave of a wand! A plastic surgeon places a digital "canvas" under a person's skin. The user can then change the display at any time thanks to some clever computer software and a special electronic "wand." For example, people can change their tattoos from a skull to a heart within seconds.

EYE-TRACKING CAMERA

The IRIS camera by designer Mimi Zou doesn't have any buttons. The camera is instead controlled by your eyes. First you focus the camera by looking through it. Then zoom in or out by squinting or opening your eyes wide. Finally, blink twice to take a picture!

SCAN TOASTER

Here's a new way to have fun in the morning. The Scan Toaster first connects to your computer to get images of text or photos. Rotating wires inside the device then burn the images onto your morning toast. Now you can eat the news when you've finished reading it!

DIET FORK

Many people believe that eating food more slowly can help with weight loss. The HAPIfork can help people to do this. This electronic utensil counts your "fork servings" per minute. When people start gulping down their dinner too quickly, HAPIfork starts flashing and vibrating to let them know that they need to slow down.

Electronic dog tag sends messages to your home computer, then Tweets to you!

PUPPY TWEETS

Imagine your phone buzzing you with the message, "I bark because I miss you." Now thanks to Puppy Tweets™, your dog can send you messages while you're away! An electronic tag on your dog's collar picks up certain sounds and movements made by your pet. The tag then sends one of 500 adorable messages to your dog's own Twitter feed.

REMOTE ANIMAL PETTER

Would you like to pet your dog while you're at school? You may soon be able to. Researchers at the National University of Singapore are using chickens to test a "tele-petting" system. First someone pets a chicken-shaped doll that contains several touch sensors. Then the sensors send signals over the Internet to a special jacket worn by a real chicken. The jacket recreates the person's touch so the chicken can feel it!

CUTTING-EDGE TOILETS

If you have a boring, normal toilet, you don't know what you're missing. Imagine relaxing to mood lighting in seven colours, foot warmers, music and air freshners. The hi-tech Numi toilet has it all. It even has a built-in **bidet** to help you feel extra fresh!

bidet *low oval basin used for washing a person's bottom area*

"CLOCKY"

This wheeled alarm clock rolls away from you to make sure you get out of bed! It beeps like a robot and can roll off of a 1-metre high surface. You never know which way it'll go, so you have to get up and look for it.

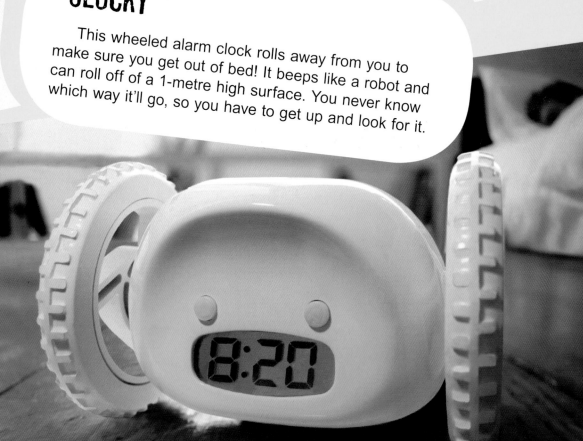

CHAPTER 3

INVENTIONS ON THE MOVE

Get ready, get set, pedal in the air! Jog on the water! Float across a continent! Throughout history people have looked for new ways to get from one place to another – and we're still attempting it today. Welcome to the amazing and very strange "inventions on the move".

AMPHIBIOUS BICYCLE

In 1975 India's Mohammed Saidullah got tired of his village being flooded every year. So he built a bicycle that he could ride both on land and in water. He added floats to the bike and put fan blades on the spokes – and it worked! Saidullah won several awards for his **ingenious** invention. However, he has yet to make any money from it.

ingenious *inventive and original*

SEA JOGGER

You can now walk on water with the Sea Jogger. First hold the handlebars and step onto the springy surface. Then start walking on the spot to move the flippers underneath. If all goes well, you will be able to walk across a nearby river – and stay dry enough to keep your shoes on!

ICY AIRCRAFT CARRIER

During World War II (1939–1945) British scientist Geoffrey Pyke came up with the idea of making an aircraft carrier out of pykrete. This incredibly tough material is made by freezing a mixture of wood pulp and water. The British government approved Pyke's idea and planned to build several pykrete ships. Unfortunately the project proved to be too expensive and the plan was scrapped.

WORLD'S SMALLEST CAR

The British Peel P50 is the world's smallest street-legal car. It is also one of the rarest vehicles in the world. Only 50 of these tiny cars were built in the 1960s, and just 27 still exist today. They have three wheels, one door and a small electric engine. At only 59 kilograms, a person can pull the Peel P50 along like a giant suitcase.

"HUMAN SPIDER-MAN" CLIMBING MACHINE

Some vacuum cleaners are more powerful than you might think. In 2010 British inventor Jem Stansfield attached vacuum cleaner hoses to two giant suction pads. He then proceeded to climb up the side of a building – just like a certain wall-crawling superhero!

HUMAN-POWERED HELICOPTER

In 1980 the American Helicopter Society issued a challenge to engineers around the world. The first team to invent a human-powered machine that could fly 3 metres high for at least one minute would win £156,000. In June 2013 a team of Canadian engineers finally nabbed the prize. Their Atlas helicopter was powered by a bike that spun four giant **propellers**.

propeller *set of rotating blades that moves a vehicle through water or air*

VACUUM-TUBE TRAINS

Scientists are currently working on technology that will allow trains to travel seven times faster than commercial jet aeroplanes. Using magnets and **vacuum tubes**, the trains would float through airless tubes at up to 6,440 kilometres an hour. There would be no wind, train tracks or road to slow down the trains. However, safety concerns and the enormous cost of building the train system are putting the brakes on this amazing idea for now.

vacuum tube *tube that has no air or other matter in it*

MONOWHEEL

In 1869 French inventor Rousseau of Marseilles, France, created one of the world's first monowheels. Riders in these vehicles roll along inside a large wheel. Monowheels are thought to offer a smoother ride than normal two-wheel bikes. Over the years there have been many different monowheel designs. So far however, the monowheels are difficult to control and can crash easily.

ROLLER SUIT

Who says roller skates are just for feet? This suit of "rolling armour" features wheels attached to a person's feet, toes, elbows, knees and more. Now you can pretend to "fly" like your favourite superhero as you roll down the road!

FACE-TO-FACE BIKE

This two-person bike has rotating seats and gears that can move in either direction. Two friends can ride sitting either face-to-face or back-to-back. Whichever way people choose to sit, the bike can still move in a forward direction.

THE REEVES OCTOAUTO

Car designers have tinkered with different car designs since cars were first invented. In 1911 Milton Reeves decided to build a new kind of car. He got his welding torch out and added four extra wheels to an Overland automobile, (a type of car produced in the United States from 1903 to 1926). Reeves claimed the OctoAuto offered a smoother ride than normal cars. It was however extremely hard to go round corners in this giant vehicle!

HORSEY HORSELESS CARRIAGE

In 1899 most people travelled in horse-drawn carriages. Cars, known then as "horseless carriages," were often a startling sight – especially for horses. But inventor Uriah Smith's Horsey Horseless vehicle was meant to solve that problem. Smith planned to place a wooden horse head on the front of a car. He thought the fake horse head would help soothe the nerves of real horses. Smith received a US patent for his idea in 1899. However, it's not known if he ever actually built this crazy car.

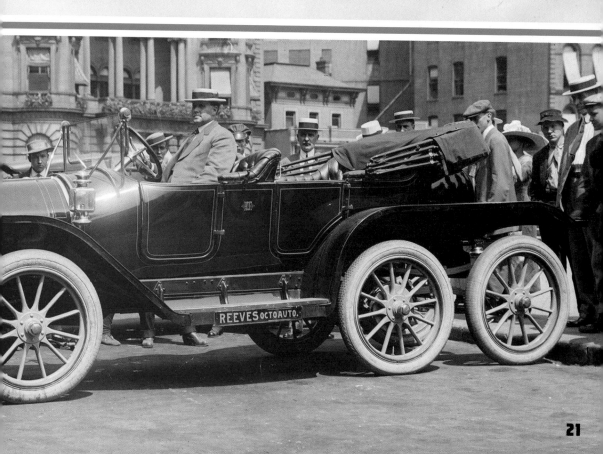

CHAPTER 4
HOW LAZY CAN YOU BE?

Without washing machines people today would still be scrubbing clothes by hand. Without the Internet people would have to spend hundreds of hours digging for information in books. Here are some other ways inventors have tried to save people time and make everyday jobs easier.

SIX-SECOND TOOTHBRUSH

The Blizzident toothbrush is uniquely designed for the person using it. This custom-made mouthpiece includes 800 bristles which sit at perfect angles to fit your teeth. Bite and grind it between your teeth between 10 and 15 times, and you will have completed your teeth brushing in just six seconds!

DEODORANT SWEETS

Why worry about putting on deodorant? Eat some sweets instead! According to the company that makes Deo Perfume Candy, eating just two to four pieces will keep you smelling rosy for up to six hours. The more you sweat, the better you'll smell!

BABY-PATTING MACHINE

It can take hours to get a baby to go to sleep. The idea behind this machine from a 1968 patent is to imitate a parent's touch. A motor-driven arm would gently pat a baby's bottom until it fell asleep, allowing parents to relax or focus on other activities.

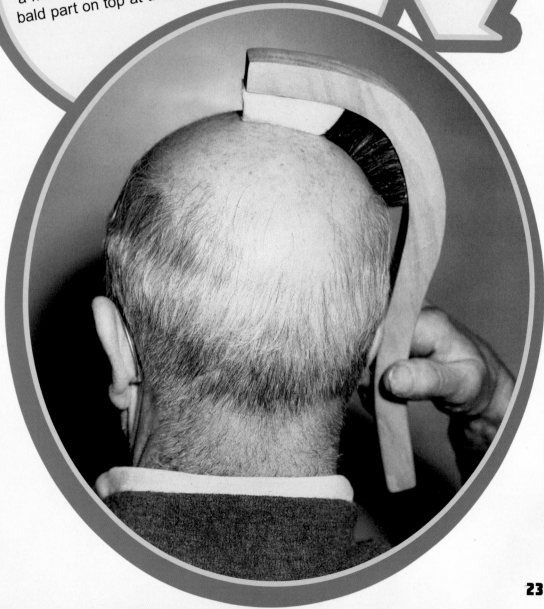

BRUSH AND SHINE

To brush or to shine? That was the question facing some men in the 1950s – until one company invented a special grooming tool to do both! It brushed a man's hair on the sides of his head while shining the bald part on top at the same time.

BOTANICALLS

Plants are a great way of adding greenery to your home. But it can be easy to forget about watering them. Now your plants can let you know when they're thirsty! The Botanicalls kit includes sensors to measure the moisture in your plant's pot. When the soil becomes too dry, it sends a message to your phone: "Water me please." After watering your plant, you'll get a nice thank-you message as well.

SNOWBALL MAKER

The Sno-Baller gently packs snow into perfect snowballs. This scooper is reported to make up to 60 snowballs a minute. As an added bonus, your hands don't even get cold or wet.

SELF-TIPPING HAT

In the late 1800s a gentleman always tipped his hat to a lady. But what if his arms were full? James C. Boyle solved this problem with a wind-up device worn under a man's hat. It could make any hat tip itself with a simple nod of the wearer's head.

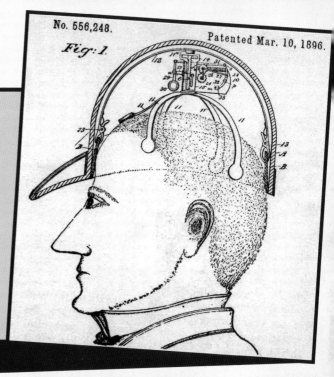

No. 556,248.

Fig: 1.

Patented Mar. 10, 1896.

SELF-STIRRING MUG

This cool gadget lets you stir your drink without hunting for a spoon. The Self-Stirring Mug has a tiny plastic disc at the bottom. Press a button to spin the disk and swirl your drink. You can even use the swirl feature to clean the mug with soapy water when you've finished.

LAZYGLASSES

Do you want to lie flat on your back to watch TV or read a book? You don't have to install a screen on the ceiling. Instead try Lazyglasses. These clever glasses use mirrors to reflect images to your eyes the same way **periscopes** do.

periscope *viewing device with mirrors at each end; periscopes are often used in submarines to see above water*

CHAPTER 5

STRANGE INVENTIONS JUST FOR KIDS

Some inventors seem to remember that being a child is all about having fun. Invent some slimy goo to play with in the bath? That's brilliant! But some inventions aren't as much fun, such as a special brush for cleaning children's necks. Which of the following inventions would earn your seal of approval?

NECK BRUSH COLLAR

Ouch! This plastic collar brush from 1950 was meant to clean a child's neck while he or she played. No soap or water was required. The brush worked when it was completely dry — unless, of course, you count the tears from the children using it.

BABY MOP

In the late 1990s the Baby Mop started as a **spoof** advertisement in Japan. But parents today can actually buy fringed outfits that turn their babies into cleaning tools! Apparently hair balls and dust stick to crawling babies better than they stick to mops.

spoof *funny imitation of something*

X-RAY SHOE FITTER

What was the best way to buy a pair of well-fitting shoes In the 1950s? By foot x-raying of course! Shoe-fitting fluoroscopes allowed shoppers to see the bones in their feet glowing inside their shoes. The machines were supposed to examine people's feet to ensure the best fitting shoes. However, the machines turned out to be a **gimmick** and exposed people to cancer-causing radiation. Most of the machines were banned by 1970.

gimmick *clever trick or idea used to gain people's attention*

GELLI BAFF

Bubble baths? How boring. Parents can now make bath time more fun with Gelli Baff! Sprinkle in a packet of "goo maker" and children's bath water turns into colourful goo. When the child has finished their bath, just mix in some "goo dissolver." The slime turns to coloured water that swirls down the drain.

BABY CAGE

City apartments can be very cramped. This was especially true in the early 1900s. In 1922 inventor Emma Read created an original solution to this problem. She invented a mesh cage for babies that was literally fixed to the outside of a window. The cage even came with a detachable, slanted roof that helped keep rain off the baby's head!

ANTI-THEFT LUNCH BAGS

Having trouble with people stealing your lunch? Here's a way to make sure they never steal your food again. These clever bags make a sandwich look mouldy and disgusting so that nobody will want to touch it. Just make sure nobody throws it away by accident!

INVENTING SUCCESS

Have you ever had an idea for an invention? Was it so strange that you thought people might laugh at you? If so, you're off to a good start! Don't let the slim chance of success put you off. Remember that many of the most successful inventions began as wonderfully weird and wacky ideas!

GLOSSARY

amplifier piece of equipment that changes sound or makes it louder

bidet low oval basin used for washing a person's bottom area

gimmick clever trick or idea used to gain people's attention

ingenious inventive and original

patent legal document giving someone sole rights to make or sell a product

periscope viewing device with mirrors at each end; periscopes are often used in submarines to see above water

propeller set of rotating blades that moves a vehicle through water or air

slogan short catchy phrase used to advertise something or to sum up an idea

spoof funny imitation of something

stylus pen-like instrument used to enter or search for information on electronic devices

vacuum tube tube that has no air or other matter in it

READ MORE

100 Inventions That Made History: Brilliant Breakthroughs that Shaped our World, Tracey Turner, (Dorling Kindersley, 2014)

Alexander Graham Bell (Science Biographies), Catherine Chambers (Raintree, 2014)

The Computer (Tales of Invention), Chris Oxlade (Heinemann Library, 2011)

WEBSITES

www.bbc.co.uk/bbcone/wallaceandgromit
Visit Wallace and Gromit's World of Invention workshop and learn how to build your own gadgets, including a balloon-powered hovercraft and a hexapod walking contraption!

www.sciencecentres.org.uk
Explore the UK Association for Science and Discovery Centres' website and find out how to get involved in exciting science workshops near you.

www.sciencemuseum.org.uk/about_us/mark_champkins
Meet the London Science Museum's Inventor in Residence, Mark Champkins, whose job it is to design new products using inspiration from inventors of the past.

INDEX